The National Trust
Centenary Souvenir

1895 – 1995

First published in 1995
by National Trust (Enterprises) Ltd
36 Queen Anne's Gate, London SW1H 9AS

© 1995 The National Trust
Registered Charity No. 205846
ISBN 0 7078 0265 2

A catalogue record for this book is available from the British Library

Text by Margaret Willes, Publisher, The National Trust

Picture research by Sheila Mortimer

Designed by Peter Guy

Production by Bob Towell

Printed and bound in Hong Kong
Mandarin Offset Limited

Title page: Blickling Hall, the Norfolk home of Lord Lothian, deviser of the Country Houses Scheme.
Front cover: Dry-stone walling, Grasmere, Cumbria.
Back cover: Kedleston Hall, Derbyshire, with the Adam fishing pavilion in the foreground.

Introduction

✦§✦

This colour souvenir has been compiled to celebrate the National Trust's centenary. To encapsulate such a huge and complex organisation in so few words is well nigh impossible, so I have chosen to highlight certain events in the Trust's life, concentrating on some of the people who have helped to shape its development, and on the properties which are its proud achievement.

For those who would like to find out more about the Trust's history, I recommend that you read Merlin Waterson's *The National Trust: the First Hundred Years,* published jointly by the National Trust and the BBC to mark the centenary.

MARGARET WILLES

The Knot Garden at Moseley Old Hall, Staffordshire. The formal garden, originally planted in 1640, has been recreated by the National Trust as it would have looked in the seventeenth century.

Founders

❦

'Mark my words, Miss Hill, this is going to be a very big thing.' This prophetic remark was made by the Duke of Westminster as plans were underway to set up the National Trust for Places of Historic Interest or Natural Beauty. The actual foundation of the Trust took place in the Duke's London home, Grosvenor House, on 12 January 1895. The three moving spirits behind this venture – Robert Hunter, Octavia Hill and Hardwicke Rawnsley – were very different: perhaps this was the secret of their success.

Robert Hunter was a skilful lawyer: as honorary Solicitor to the Commons Preservation Society, he fought important battles to save common lands and forests from enclosure. Octavia Hill had gained an international reputation with her housing schemes for the poor of London, first in Marylebone, later in the East End.

In 1874, Octavia Hill and Robert Hunter launched an appeal to save Swiss Cottage Fields in north London from building development. Although the money was raised, the land was lost and both realised that an organisation was urgently required that could acquire properties to ensure permanent preservation.

The third founder was Hardwicke Rawnsley, vicar of Wray on Windermere, Cumberland. He became deeply concerned that the unspoilt beauty of the Lakes would be lost to posterity. Almost a century earlier, the poet William Wordsworth had declared that the Lake District should be 'a sort of national property in which every man has a right and interest, who has an eye to perceive and a heart to enjoy'. Canon Rawnsley carried this through by combining with Robert Hunter and Octavia Hill to found the National Trust in 1895.

Sir Robert Hunter
towards the end of his life.
He died in 1913.

Octavia Hill,
a copy of John Singer Sargent's portrait,
painted to celebrate her 60th birthday
in 1898.

Hardwicke Rawnsley
photographed in 1907 at Lingholm
in the Lake District.

Sources of Inspiration

The founders of the National Trust received support and inspiration from a whole host of people, many distinguished names amongst them. At the Commons Preservation Society, Robert Hunter worked closely with reforming politicians like Charles Shaw-Lefevre and Sir Charles Dilke, and Thomas Hughes, author of *Tom Brown's Schooldays*. Octavia Hill's early mentor was Rev. F.D. Maurice, spiritual leader of the Christian Socialists, and one of the most controversial and influential theologians of the nineteenth century. Charles Dickens and the philanthropic millionairess Angela Burdett-Coutts inspired her housing reform work. Hardwicke Rawnsley was much influenced by the poetic vision of William Wordsworth and Samuel Taylor Coleridge.

But perhaps the strongest source of inspiration came from John Ruskin – artist, critic, teacher, philosopher and social reformer. Octavia Hill first met him in 1853, when she began to work as his picture copyist. She expressed the lyrical hope that 'well-used, this friendship, so happily begun, may be a long and glowing one'. The road ahead was not to prove so smooth, but Ruskin at this time provided the financial support to enable her to start up her housing improvement schemes.

When Hardwicke Rawnsley was an undergraduate at Oxford, he became a member of Ruskin's Hinksey road-mending gang, as did that unlikeliest of all navvies, Oscar Wilde. Rawnsley told Ruskin of his interest in undertaking social work in London, and was thus introduced to Octavia Hill, whom Ruskin described as 'the best lady abbess you can find for London work'.

In 1871 Ruskin set up the Guild of St George to acquire land to be cultivated or turned into common land, to provide schools, and to build museums in which the best works of God and man might be exhibited. But he was not a practical man on financial matters, and Octavia Hill was rash enough to point this out to him, causing the quarrel which was to sour their relationship for many years. Reconciliation came in 1897, but by this time Ruskin was a pathetic and disillusioned man. When he died three years later, Rawnsley proposed a memorial for him on Friar's Crag, overlooking Derwentwater in the Lake District, with his portrait in bronze relief on a piece of Borrowdale slate.

John Ruskin, a portrait by John Everett Millais, 1853.
This is a poignant painting, as Millais had travelled to Glenfinlas in Scotland
with Ruskin and his wife, Effie. He duly painted the portrait but also fell in love with Effie,
who married him after divorcing Ruskin.

Historic Buildings

❧

The National Trust's first historic building was the fourteenth-century clergy house at Alfriston in Sussex. The local vicar, the Rev. F.W. Beynon, had been fighting to save the dilapidated timber-framed house from demolition. Having tried several lines of rescue, he alighted upon Canon Rawnsley and the house was duly transferred from the Ecclesiastical Commissioners to the National Trust in April 1896 for the nominal sum of £10. The repair bill would prove much higher. True to the precepts of Ruskin, Octavia Hill wrote, 'we should very naturally be asked to "restore" it, in so far as that odious word means preservation from decay'. With the help of the Society for the Protection of Ancient Buildings (SPAB), the Trust inaugurated a modest programme of the most vital repairs: it had perforce to be modest, amounting to £150, as the Trust's income was tiny, around £300 per annum. The less vital was put off until later.

Octavia Hill, in a speech made a few years later, explains why she and her colleagues were so keen to preserve vernacular buildings of the countryside: 'our small houses, steep in roof and gable, mellowed with the colour of ages, picturesque in outline, rich in memories of England as our ancestors knew it: Alfriston, pre-Reformation clergy house nestled below the Sussex Downs; Long Crendon Court-house, used since the time of Henry V, standing at the end of the long street of a needle-making village of Oxfordshire; the old post office at Tintagel, a picturesque fourteenth-century cottage . . .'.

In 1907, the Trust took on a much more substantial historical building, sixteenth-century Barrington Court in Somerset. The house was in a poor state of repair, but a benefactor came forward. In the long term, even this support proved inadequate, and Barrington has always been a drain on funds. The experience was to cast a long shadow over the Trust's decisions on country houses – thirty years later a former Secretary of the National Trust was still heard to invoke the memory of Barrington Court should such a potential acquisition be proposed.

Above: Barrington Court, Somerset: the National Trust's first country house.
Below: Alfriston Clergy House in Sussex, bought by the Trust in 1896 for £10.

Coast

❦

'I have long wanted to secure for the public for ever the enjoyment of Dinas Oleu, but I wish to put it into the custody of some society that will never vulgarise it, or prevent wild nature from having its own way . . . I wish to avoid the abomination of asphalt paths and the cast-iron seats of serpent design.'

With these words, Fanny Talbot presented the National Trust with its first property, a matter of weeks after its formation in 1895. Hardwicke Rawnsley was staying with Mrs Talbot at Barmouth on the Welsh coast when the draft articles of association were sent to him by the Trust's solicitors. A friend of Ruskin, Mrs Talbot was quick to see the potential of the infant organisation: 'I perceive your Trust will be of the greatest use to me.'

Her gift of Dinas Oleu was 4.5 acres of steep, gorse-clad rocky fell above Barmouth, with striking views over Cardigan Bay. By giving this fragment of land, Mrs Talbot prevented the spread of development along the coast: the great sadness is that there were not more Mrs Talbots preserving other seaside towns in the same way at this key time.

Other coastal acquisitions followed. In 1897 Barras Nose in Tintagel in Cornwall was bought by subscription. Noting the connection with King Arthur, Hardwicke Rawnsley recorded poetically its 'soft grass, enamelled with great patches of thyme . . . and golden with anthyllis'. In 1925, the Farne Islands off the Northumbrian coast, an important breeding site for seabirds, were also acquired after an appeal, and two years later, 150 acres of cliff land on the Isle of Wight were presented to the Trust by the 2nd Lord Tennyson in memory of his father, the Poet Laureate.

Barras Nose, looking towards Tintagel in Cornwall, the first piece of English coastline bought by the National Trust, in 1897. This area held particular charms for Hardwicke Rawnsley because of Arthurian associations, but it was hard-headed anticipation of housing developments that persuaded the Trust to acquire the land.

Countryside

❧

Early National Trust acquisitions reflect the enthusiasms of the founders. Octavia Hill, her family and friends acquired and presented land around Toys Hill in Kent. As Octavia pointed out: 'Here promontories are very rapidly purchased for building and enclosed.'

Robert Hunter, recalling youthful holidays, was determined to preserve the greensand ridge at Hindhead in Surrey, along the south-facing scarp of the North Downs. In 1906, the Hindhead Preservation Society, nudged along by Hunter, gave the Trust 750 acres embracing the Devil's Punchbowl, followed two years later by Ludshott Common.

In 1902 the National Trust acquired its first property in the Lake District, the woods and parkland at Brandelhow on the west side of Derwentwater. Factory workers in northern cities responded to the appeal launched by Canon Rawnsley. One female worker from Sheffield sent Octavia Hill 2/6d with the poignant message: 'All my life I have longed to see the Lakes . . . I shall never see them now, but I should like to keep them for others.'

In 1907 Robert Hunter drew up legislation for a National Trust Act to go through Parliament, taking many of the clauses from the original articles of association. The Act made clear the Trust's first duty, to hold places of natural beauty or historic interest in permanent preservation for the benefit of the nation. Of all the powers conferred on the Trust by this Act, the most important is the right to hold land inalienably. Once land is thus declared, it cannot be sold or mortgaged or compulsorily acquired against the Trust's wishes without Special Parliamentary Procedure.

Derwentwater in Cumbria, from the lower slopes of Catbells
with Brandelhow in the foreground. When an appeal was launched to buy land at
Brandelhow in 1902, Octavia Hill described the site: 'a mile of lakeshore, views of Skiddaw
in one direction and Borrowdale in the other, from its slope you can see the whole space of
the lake set with its islands.'

Nature Reserves

The concept of the Trust acquiring nature reserves was first brought up at a meeting on 26 April 1895 when Herbert Goss, a distinguished entomologist, suggested that the then very infant organisation should consider saving Wicken Fen in Cambridgeshire, the only substantial area of East Anglian fenland still undrained. A mere 17 miles north-west of Cambridge, it was a haunt of moth and butterfly hunters, who were threatening to destroy the habitat by their enthusiasm. In 1879 the massed lamps of the collectors made the Fen look as if it were illuminated by street lights, according to one complaint. A fellow entomologist, J.C. Moberley, sold a two-acre strip of the Fen to the National Trust in 1899 for £10, and more portions were added over the years so that the Trust now owns over 600 acres, and in 1993 Wicken Fen was finally recognised as a national nature reserve.

Today the National Trust has over 70 sites which it regards as nature reserves, and 339 Sites of Special Scientific Interest. Blakeney Point on the north Norfolk coast and the Farne Islands in Northumberland are both sanctuaries for seabirds. The smallest SSSI in Britain is a colony of horseshoe bats that lives in the roof-space of the old stable block at Stackpole in Dyfed.

When Calke Abbey in Derbyshire was acquired by the Trust in 1985, newspaper headlines concentrated on the fact that it was a time capsule thanks to the eccentric lifestyle of the Harpur Crewe family who have lived there since the seventeenth century. Hardly remarked upon in all the excitement was the family's other enduring quality, their love of natural history. The park is one of the best in Britain for insects, mainly beetles. The woodland is the relict of Derbyshire forest cover dating back to *c*.5000 BC, and the species are direct descendants of the original 'wildwood' fauna that has survived as a result of unbroken continuity. Calke Abbey thus joins the many important nature reserves in the National Trust's care.

Reed-cutting at Wicken Fen, Cambridgeshire.

Beatrix Potter

Beatrix Potter was familiar with the work of the National Trust from the outset. From 1882 her family spent their summer holidays at Wray Castle on Windermere and here she met Canon Rawnsley, who encouraged her artistic talents and instilled in her the importance of conservation.

In 1905, using the royalties from *The Tale of Peter Rabbit* and her other children's books, she bought Hill Top at Near Sawrey, a Cumbrian farmhouse with 34 acres of

working land. A manager was installed in an extension to the house, and she travelled up from London for frequent visits. But her ties with the Lake District tightened as her literary output relaxed. William Heelis, a local solicitor, kept her informed of further properties coming on the market, and in 1913 they married, moving into Castle Farm, also in Near Sawrey.

Troutbeck Park Farm, a spectacular site of more than 1,000 acres, was bought in 1924, and Beatrix Potter subsequently ran the farm herself with the help of a shepherd, Tom Storey. Together they built up a flock of Herdwick sheep, and Beatrix Potter became President of the Herdwick Sheepbreeders Association, founded half a century earlier by Hardwicke Rawnsley.

In 1929 one of the most magnificent Lake District estates came up for sale: Monk Coniston, with 2,500 acres around the head of Coniston Water, including Tarn Hows, 7 farms, cottages, quarries and open fells. Beatrix Potter bought the whole estate, sold half to the National Trust and for the next ten years acted as their agent, in almost daily correspondence with the London office and expressing herself in forthright terms. Although often critical of the Trust, she never wavered in her support, commenting philosophically: 'The Trust is a noble thing and humanly speaking immortal. There are some silly mortals connected with it, but they will pass.' At her death in 1943 she bequeathed 4,000 acres of land, farmhouses and cottages in the Lake District to the National Trust.

Winter at Tarn Hows, on the Monk Coniston estate, Cumbria.
Left: Peter Rabbit, on the run from Mr McGregor, takes refuge in a watering can.
One of Beatrix Potter's illustrations for *The Tale of Peter Rabbit*, published in 1902.

George Macaulay Trevelyan

❧

'George is an historian of the most superior sort
He knows more facts in history than anybody ought'

The subject of this verse, by his daughter Mary, was George Macaulay Trevelyan, Master of Trinity College, Cambridge, Regius Professor of Modern History at Cambridge, and, through his many books, probably the widest-read historian of his generation. He was also an influential benefactor of the National Trust.

He was born in 1876, the youngest son of George Otto Trevelyan of Wallington in Northumberland. His first connection with the Trust came in 1912 when he wrote to *The Times* in support of an appeal to acquire the Roman fort at Ambleside in the Lake District, an area he loved and knew well. Thirteen years later he took part in another National Trust appeal, this time to save several thousand acres of the Ashridge Estate in Hertfordshire. Enlisting the support of no fewer than three British Prime Ministers – Stanley Baldwin, Ramsay MacDonald and Herbert Asquith – Ashridge was duly acquired.

As Chairman of the Trust's Estate Committee in the 1930s, he was instrumental in securing countryside properties all over England, including parts of Hadrian's Wall in his native Northumberland. He also anticipated Enterprise Neptune: in a letter to the Trust's Secretary in January 1931 he suggested a survey should be carried out to identify stretches of unspoilt coastline which might be acquired before they came on the open market. More than thirty years were to pass before such a scheme came into effect (p.38).

In 1929 G.M.Trevelyan encapsulated his passionately held philosophy about conservation of the countryside, and of the buildings in it, in *Must England's Beauty Perish?*: 'without vision the people perish, and without natural beauty the English people will perish in the spiritual sense'.

Wallington estate in Northumberland, family home of the Trevelyans.

Archaeology

❧

The preservation of ancient monuments was not a specific intention of the National Trust's founders, but open spaces acquired for their landscape inevitably contained monuments of national importance. The first, White Barrow, a Neolithic long barrow near Tilshead in Wiltshire, was bought in 1909.

The interconnection between ancient monument and landscape embroiled the Trust in the most famous archaeological site in England, Stonehenge. After several alarums and excursions, the great stone circle was presented to the State in 1918, passing first to the Office of Works, later to the Department of Environment and English Heritage. In the 1920s, however, the surrounding landscape was under threat of development, and following a national appeal led by Stanley Baldwin, the Trust acquired Stonehenge Down. Stonehenge remains in the eye of the storm, with plans to re-route major roads away from the stones and to improve the visitor experience the subjects of bitter and unresolved debate.

Over the years the National Trust has acquired many important monuments, including Avebury in Wiltshire, Chedworth Roman Villa in Gloucestershire and parts of Hadrian's Wall in Northumberland. The dilemma has always been whether the Trust held these sites for their romance and beauty or for conservation. In 1949 the distinguished historian Professor Ian Richmond argued that these sites should be explored and protected, and as a result several were put under the guardianship of the Office of Works.

Out of this debate, the Trust has evolved a philosophy towards its ancient monuments. By using the power of inalienability, it has been able to preserve its monuments when modern development has meant the destruction of sites elsewhere. Professional archaeologists on the staff have carried out investigations where necessary, from excavating the Victorian garden at Biddulph Grange in Staffordshire to surveying the medieval timbered buildings at Little Moreton Hall in Cheshire.

The prehistoric Megalithic circle at Castlerigg, Cumbria, one of the first archaeological monuments bought by the National Trust, in 1913.

Ferguson's Gang

❧

'A fully masked woman, burdened with a sack, presented herself to the astonished and somewhat tremulous Secretary. It was soon seen that this was no masked bandit, but a benefactor. The sack was deposited on the Secretary's table and found to contain no less than £100 in silver coins.' This extraordinary story comes from *The Times*, 1 February 1933: the Secretary was Samuel Hamer, the 'scene of the crime' the National Trust's headquarters in Buckingham Palace Gate, and the masked intruder was 'Red Biddy' of Ferguson's Gang.

The gang was founded in 1927, according to a later report in the *Evening News* 'by a young Society woman who, after a brilliant career at Cambridge University, came to King's College [London] and banded her friends together'. Clough Williams-Ellis had just published *England & the Octopus*, a warning against the spread of urbanisation and despoliation of the countryside that had taken place in the few years since the end of the First World War. The first law of the gang, therefore, was 'to follow the precepts of Ferguson in preserving England and frustrating the octopus'.

Masking themselves behind pseudonyms like Bloody Bishop, Bill Stickers, Sister Agatha and See Mee Run, the gang made their first gift to the National Trust in 1932 with the purchase of Shalford Mill, an eighteenth-century watermill outside Guildford in Surrey. The gang went on to give the Old Town Hall in Newtown, Isle of Wight, Priory Cottages at Steventon in Oxfordshire, and Mayon and Trevescan cliffs between Sennon Cove and Land's End in Cornwall: a total of £3,500 and contributions to fourteen separate appeals. Ferguson's Gang dispersed towards the end of the 1930s; their identities still remain a mystery.

Shalford Mill, an eighteenth-century watermill near Guildford in Surrey.
Ferguson's Gang bought the mill for the National Trust in 1932, and used it
as their meeting place, sitting around one of the grindstones.

Country Houses

One of the prevailing conceptions of the National Trust today is of an organisation that looks after stately homes. Thus it comes as quite a surprise to realise that until the mid-1930s the Trust owned only two sizeable country houses, Barrington Court (p.8) and Montacute, both in Somerset.

At the National Trust AGM on 19 July 1934, Philip Kerr, Marquess of Lothian made a speech which turned out to mark a watershed: 'The country houses of Britain . . . are under sentence of death, and the axe which is destroying them is taxation and especially that form of taxation known as death duties.'

Lothian went on to devise the Country Houses Scheme, whereby the National Trust could accept country houses and estates in lieu of death duties, with the proviso that an endowment in the form of land or money should also be given to provide for maintenance. Parliament passed the required new legislation in the form of two National Trust Acts of 1937 and 1939.

A Historic Country Houses Committee was appointed with James Lees-Milne acting as Secretary. He drew up a list of houses and proceeded to visit their owners, a process memorably recorded in his diaries. Perhaps one of the most vivid descriptions is of his visit to Sir Henry and Lady Hoare at Stourhead in Wiltshire in October 1942: 'Sir Henry is an astonishing 19th-century John Bull, hobbling on two sticks . . . Lady Hoare is an absolute treasure . . . in a long black skirt belled from a wasp waist. The Hoares have reigned 50 years here. Their only son was killed in the last war and both of them live on his memory.' Five years later Stourhead, with its great collection of art and wonderful landscape garden (p.32) passed to the Trust.

The first house to come to the National Trust under the Country Houses Scheme had been the fascinating Arts and Crafts Wightwick Manor in Staffordshire, given by Sir Geoffrey and Lady Mander. All too soon Lord Lothian's own home, the Jacobean jewel of Blickling Hall in Norfolk, followed as a result of his premature death in 1940.

The Great Parlour at Wightwick Manor, West Midlands,
with William Morris's 'Diagonal Trail' woven wool on the walls below the frieze
and Edward Burne-Jones's painting of *Love among the Ruins*.

Great Collections

❧

The Country Houses Scheme (p.24) brought to the National Trust not only houses of importance but also their contents. The 1937 Parliament Act stated that the Trust's purposes should be extended to include 'the preservation of furniture and pictures and chattels of every description, having national or historic or artistic interest'. Today the Trust looks after 8,000 oil paintings, 100,000 drawings, watercolours and engravings, 1,000 sculptures, 30,000 ceramics and glass items, and 50,000 books.

Of all the National Trust's houses, Knole in Kent has perhaps the best claim to be called a palace. Home of the medieval Archbishops of Canterbury, it was reluctantly presented by Thomas Cranmer to Henry VIII in 1538. Twenty years later Knole was granted to Thomas Sackville and remained with his family for four hundred years. During this time the historic contents were gathered, spectacularly enhanced by Charles Sackville, 6th Earl of Dorset. As Lord Chamberlain to William III, he was able to claim as perquisites from the royal palaces beds and chairs of state, a magnificent set of Brussels tapestries, and a unique collection of seventeenth-century silver furniture.

The house where collections reign supreme is Snowshill Manor in Gloucestershire. Charles Paget Wade bought the Cotswold manor house in 1919 and filled it with what appears a curiously eclectic collection, of painted European furniture, bicycles, kitchen bygones and Japanese warrior costumes. There was method behind his acqusitions, however. In 1945 he explained: 'I have not bought things because they were rare or valuable, there are many things of everyday use in the past of small value, but of interest as records of various vanished handicrafts.' Reserving the manor for his collections, Wade moved into an adjacent cottage, the Priest's House, but even this is filled with objects.

Pieces from the collection of seventeenth-century silver furniture in the
King's Bedroom at Knole in Kent.

People & Places

To Hardwicke Rawnsley, the spirit of the place was a vital quality, and particularly any personal connections. When Minchinhampton Common in Gloucestershire was bought in 1913 to stop quarrying there, he transcended the prosaic to recall, 'hereabouts, in 628, Penda King of Mercia fought a bloody fight against his two rebellious sons, Cynegills and Cwichelm'.

The Trust's first house connected with a famous person was Coleridge's Cottage at Nether Stowey in Somerset, bought in 1909. Coleridge had moved into the tiny cottage with his wife and baby son in 1796, and there wrote *The Ancient Mariner*. But it was not until 1936 that the Trust really determined to collect buildings with special connections, acquiring them at the rate of about one a year until 1950: for example, Carlyle's House in Chelsea, London; Ellen Terry's Smallhythe Place in Kent; T.E.Lawrence's Clouds Hill in Dorset.

In 1943 G.B.Shaw wrote a characteristically forthright letter to the Trust offering his house in Ayot St Lawrence in Hertfordshire at his death: 'I am in my 87th year and about to make my last will. Has such a trifle any use or interest …?' When he died in 1950 the Trust found itself with a house and no endowment, and villagers worrying about crowds on their doorsteps, although the visitor numbers have in fact always been low.

In striking contrast, there are two Trust houses connected with famous people that have proved a great attraction. Tens of thousands of visitors make the annual pilgrimage to Beatrix Potter's Hill Top in Near Sawrey, Cumbria, to see the place where she worked on her 'little books' (p.16). Chartwell in Kent became the Churchill family home in 1924. Despite his political prominence and prodigious output of writings, Winston Churchill was always short of money. Matters came to a head in 1945, and a group of friends responded by buying Chartwell from Churchill and presenting it to the Trust, subject to the right of Mr and Mrs Churchill to occupy it in their lifetimes. At his death in 1965, Lady Churchill handed the house over to the National Trust as a permanent and personal memorial to her husband.

Churchill's chair at Chartwell. Here he liked to paint, and feed the golden orfe in the pool.

Winston Churchill's Library at Chartwell, Kent, with a relief model of Port Arromanches in Normandy as it appeared on 23 September 1944.

Gardens

'After luncheon, Laurie Johnston took me aside to ask if the National Trust would take over Hidcote Garden without endowment after the War.' So ran James Lees-Milne's diary entry for 5 February 1943, marking another new departure for the Trust, the acquisition of gardens for their own sake, as opposed to appendages to houses.

Lawrence Johnston had arrived at Hidcote in Gloucestershire in 1907 and, despite having no previous gardening experience, proceeded to create over the next thirty years a great garden, with its blend of ordered formality and apparent artlessness of the cottage garden. Johnston was also developing a garden in the south of France, La Serre de la Madonne, and wanted to live there permanently. His mother had left him only a life interest in her estate at her death in 1926, hence the lack of an endowment. Nevertheless the National Trust took on Hidcote in 1948.

In this same year, Lord Aberconway, President of the Royal Horticultural Society, had set up a joint committee of the RHS and the National Trust to raise money for the administration of the 'best gardens of England'. As a result, the National Trust soon acquired several important gardens, not all of them 'of England'. In 1949 Lord Aberconway entrusted nearly 100 acres of his garden at Bodnant in North Wales to the National Trust. In the same year Lady Londonderry enquired about the Trust taking over the garden she had created at Mount Stewart in Northern Ireland, a transfer that took place in 1955. Phyllis Reiss's beautiful garden at Tintinhull in Somerset was given in 1953, and in 1967 the famous garden at Sissinghurst Castle, created by Vita Sackville-West and Harold Nicolson, was transferred to the Trust.

Today the National Trust looks after more than 130 important gardens, including, taken together, the largest collection of cultivated plants in the world.

Right: The strea near Ladies Wall Mount Stewart, Co. Down, part of the lovely gar created by Lady Londonderry from 1921.

The Rose Borde Lawrence Johns famous garden a Hidcote Manor, Gloucestershire, wisteria, allium and lilac.

Historical Gardens

꧁❦꧂

In 1948, when Lord Aberconway called upon the National Trust to acquire and adminis-ter 'the best gardens of England' (p.30), he was thinking principally of gardens of horti-cultural importance. Nevertheless, the Trust at this very time was taking on gardens which lived up to the criterion of 'historic interest' as well as 'natural beauty'.

When Sir Henry and Lady Hoare died on the same day, Lady Day 1947, they left to the Trust the superb landscape garden at Stourhead in Wiltshire, created by Henry Hoare II. The 'natural landscape', dotted with classical eye-catchers like the Pantheon and the Temple of Apollo, presents an English eighteenth-century view of Arcadian paradise.

Other great landscape gardens followed: Claremont in Surrey, landscaped by Sir John Vanbrugh, Charles Bridgeman, William Kent and 'Capability' Brown; Studley Royal in Yorkshire, an early eighteenth-century 'green' garden; Rievaulx Terrace, also in York-shire, laid out in 1758 to provide views of the medieval abbey in the valley below; and Stowe, perhaps the supreme example of landscape gardening, laid out by the four garden-ers who had worked at Claremont. In addition, the Trust owns many parkland landscapes by 'Capability' Brown and Humphry Repton including Repton's personal favourite, Sheringham on the north Norfolk coast.

The National Trust has also restored a whole series of historical gardens, ranging from an evocation of an Elizabethan nuttery, orchard and herb garden at Hardwick Hall in Derbyshire, through formal knot gardens at Ham House, Surrey, and Moseley Old Hall, Staffordshire (p.3), to the peak of Victorian gardening, Biddulph Grange, also in Staffordshire. Historical varieties of apples are to be seen – and occasionally tasted – at Berrington Hall in Hereford & Worcester, and local varieties of vegetables at the garden of the Apprentice House at Styal, Cheshire. At Clumber Park in Nottinghamshire, the kitchen gardens that supplied the grandiloquent Victorian household have been restored and there is even a museum of nineteenth-century kitchen gardening in the vineries.

Moon pools and the Temple of Piety at Studley Royal, Yorkshire.
This formal water garden was laid out from 1716 by John Aislabie.

Estates

◆∘§∘◆

In March 1937 Sir Charles Trevelyan took the unusual step of announcing his intention of leaving his estate of Wallington in Northumberland to the National Trust in a radio broadcast. He announced in ringing tones: 'As a Socialist, I am not hampered by any sentiment of ownership. I am prompted to act as I am doing by satisfaction at knowing that the place I love will be held in perpetuity for the people of my country.'

Sir Charles was familiar with the National Trust as his youngest brother was G.M.Trevelyan (p.18). He was also a friend of Philip Kerr, Lord Lothian, who launched his idea of the Country Houses Scheme (p.24) in a stirring speech on 19 July 1934: 'the country houses of Britain, with their gardens, their parks, their pictures, their furniture, their peculiar ancestral charm represent a treasure of great beauty which is not only specially characteristic but quite unrivalled in any other land.'

Wallington fitted this precisely: Sir Charles was proposing to hand over 13,000 acres, including the late seventeenth-century house and its contents, the garden and park, the village of Cambo and 23 working farms. The Trust, then a very small organisation, was overawed by the sheer size, but a Deed of Settlement was signed in 1941 whereby Sir Charles owned and managed his estate during his lifetime; thereafter it was the Trust's.

By the time of Sir Charles's death in 1958 the Trust had acquired several estates, including West Wycombe in Buckinghamshire, Charlecote in Warwickshire and Sir Richard Acland's huge gift of Holnicote and Killerton in Somerset and Devon respectively. In only 16 years, the Trust had taken on 85,000 acres, a heavy responsibility which obliged it to move into a higher gear of management. However, had the Trust not done so, many great estates would have been broken up and their distinctive character, so lyrically described by Lothian, lost for ever.

A late medieval, traditional farmhouse on the Killerton estate, Devon.
This house is now divided into three National Trust holiday cottages.

Industrial Archaeology

Archaeological sites came early to the National Trust (p.20) but industrial monuments did not receive sympathetic treatment until the arrival of John Smith on the scene. Sir Harold Nicolson in a letter to his wife Vita in 1952 records John Smith's introduction to the Trust's Historic Buildings Committee. This body, he wrote, composed largely of peers, hoped such a proletarian name might leaven the mixture, but rapture was speedily modified when it transpired he was the brother-in-law of the Earl of Euston.

John Smith provided not only a proletarian name to Trust committees but also an original mind and financial acumen: through his Landmark and Manifold Trusts he has proved a generous supporter of many National Trust acquisitions. A fascination for feats of engineering galvanised him into a drive to save Britain's canals, under severe threat in the late 1950s: 'When the Trust was formed, there was no thought of our owning large numbers of country houses or gardens; but when the need arose, we met it; let us now take another step forward and come to the rescue of a third sort of property . . . at once a source of pleasure and a manifestation of English genius.'

In 1959 the Trust took on the lease of the Stratford-on-Avon Canal. Other initiatives shortly followed: Thomas Telford's Conwy Suspension Bridge in North Wales; beam engines, remains of Cornwall's mining industry; and with financial help from the Landmark Trust, a beetling mill – for the final process of linen manufacture – at Wellbrook in County Tyrone, Northern Ireland.

Aberdulais Falls in the Vale of Neath was given to the Trust in 1981, and a major conservation programme was instituted. Waterpower has been harnessed here for 400 years: for copper smelting in Tudor times; for an eighteenth-century corn mill to feed the growing towns of the Welsh valleys; and for a Victorian tin plate works. Today the water wheel and power generation programme provide renewable, environmentally friendly electricity.

Ronnie Alford, one of the 'greasy gang',
working on the Levant engine
in Cornwall.

Aberdulais Falls, West Glamorgan. Now a local beauty spot,
this was once an important industrial site, with a whole series
of enterprises harnessing the water power of the falls.

Enterprise Neptune

❧

In 1964 the National Trust owned 187 miles of unspoilt coastline, including its most recent acquisition, the spectacular Giant's Causeway on the Antrim coast of Northern Ireland.

However, concern was being expressed about the fate of Britain's coastline. The National Trust had conducted a survey in 1963 to look at the 3,000 miles that make up the coastline of England, Wales and Northern Ireland. Some land was already protected by the Trust and other conservation organisations: of the rest, one-third was deemed to have been developed beyond conservation, one-third was considered of little interest, but one-third was reckoned to be of outstanding natural beauty and worthy of preservation. As a result, Enterprise Neptune was launched by the National Trust in spring 1965. Its aim was to secure for the Trust the 1,000 miles of coastline of outstanding beauty, a unique project in that it is the only area where the Trust is *actively* campaigning to acquire property.

Enterprise Neptune has proved tremendously successful, both in terms of income – about £1 million each year – and of acquisition of land. In 1988, a halfway mark was reached with the purchase of the 500th mile, the coal-blackened beach at Easington in County Durham from British Coal for the sum of £1. Easington would not have appeared on the original list, for it could in no way represent outstanding beauty, but the area between cliffs and high-water mark contains a whole series of very important natural habitats.

Another property that might not have passed muster in the 1963 survey is Orford Ness, bought from the Ministry of Defence in 1993, with Neptune contributing £600,000. The 5-mile stretch of shingle running parallel with the Suffolk coast proved the ideal place for twentieth-century military research. Many of the buildings connected with these activities remain, adding powerfully to the mournful beauty of this, the most important shingle spit cuspate foreland complex in England.

Drainage dykes on Orford Ness, Suffolk. In the distance can be seen some of the remains of the Cobra Mist, 'over the horizon radar', site.

Social History

✦§✦

In 1973, the National Trust took on another country house, Erddig in Clwyd. It already owned many historic houses, but Erddig was different. The seventeenth-century house had been for two and a half centuries the home of the Yorke family. The Yorkes can be neatly divided into two categories: the Simons were decent and rather dull, the Philips were also decent, but far from dull. Throughout the years at Erddig, they enjoyed a remarkable rapport with their servants, commissioning their portraits, writing poems in their honour, and preserving their correspondence alongside inventories and account books, giving a vivid social record of life.

When the last of the Yorkes, Philip III, inherited in 1966, Erddig had suffered over half a century of decay, hastened by undermining from collieries: one of the Trust's staff, when he first visited, described 'the death mask of a house which faced two vast slag heaps in the park'. Despite the terrible state of the property, the National Trust agreed to take it on, and to use the huge quantity of housekeeping accounts to guide not only the restoration, but how it might be explained to visitors. The visitor route started not, as usual, through the front door, but through the estate, stable and laundry yards, so that visitors should imagine themselves as valet or lady's maid rather than honoured guests.

This was how Erddig was shown when it was opened to the public in 1979, and the approach has proved enormously successful. It has also provided two knock-on effects: the Trust shows its kitchens, laundries and nurseries, as well as the great state rooms; and properties are acquired that represent the social history of ordinary people – for example, Oakhurst Cottage in Surrey, the Apprentice House at Styal Mill in Lancashire, and the Fen Cottage at Wicken in Cambridgeshire.

Above: Indoor staff at Erddig, Clwyd, in a photograph taken in 1924 to celebrate the coming of age of Simon Yorke IV, the penultimate owner of the estate.
Below: Pieces of the copper *batterie de cuisine* hanging in the kitchen at Erddig.

7 Blyth Grove & 2 Willow Road

◆§₹◆

Two ordinary addresses, two less than ordinary National Trust properties. No 7 Blyth Grove is a semi-detached Edwardian house in Worksop, Nottinghamshire. In 1923 it became the home of the Straw family: William, a successful Worksop grocer, his wife Florence, and two sons, William and Walter.

In 1932 William senior died suddenly, a blow so devastating that the family allowed nothing to change from that day forward: even the calendar on the wall of the dining-room still marks that year. The process of embalming was complete with Florence's death seven years later. While other houses around were 'improved', refurbished or demolished, No 7 remained frozen in time until 1990 when William junior, last of the Straws, died. Although not a member, he left the contents of the house and nearly £1 million to the National Trust. William no doubt would have been amazed at the Trust's decision to preserve Blyth Grove as a social document of middle-class life of the 1920s and '30s.

In complete contrast stands 2 Willow Road in Hampstead, north London. This was the creation of Modern Movement architect Erno Goldfinger. In 1938, to the horror of his neighbours, he demolished a row of eighteenth-century cottages and built instead a terrace of three houses, taking the middle one as his family home. He applied in the design the principles he was to employ in major post-war commissions: reinforced concrete relieved by brick facing but avoiding the use of any unnecessary mouldings. The interior was designed down to the smallest detail and filled with paintings and sculpture by Modern Movement artists including Max Ernst and Henry Moore.

In 1994 the Trust took the bold step of acquiring 2 Willow Road, at the time of writing its most modern historic building.

Above: Erno Goldfinger's interior perspective at 2 Willow Road, Hampstead.
Below: Part of the Parlour of Mr Straw's House at 7 Blyth Grove,
Worksop in Nottinghamshire.

Sutton House

❧

To many, the National Trust is essentially a countryside organisation. It comes therefore as quite a surprise to find that the Trust owns a Tudor building, Sutton House in Hackney, east London.

When Ralph Sadleir, courtier and civil servant, built himself a fine brick, H-shaped house in 1535, Hackney was the favoured resort of courtiers and merchants. But Hackney moved on from a village on the outskirts of the City to a clerkly suburb, and finally a deprived inner-city community.

The house was acquired by the National Trust in 1936. Surviving Hitler's bombs, it was used as offices until 1982 when, after the abrupt departure of the last tenants, first squatters, then vandals and thieves moved in. The Trust, in desperation, decided to transfer the house on a long lease for conversion into residential units. The local community thought otherwise, and persuaded the Trust to reverse this decision and institute a programme of repair and refurbishment.

Today, Sutton House positively throbs with activity, with local residents as well as visitors using the café/bar and shop. Concerts, conferences, craft fairs all take place, even in the Tudor panelled rooms which have been sturdily furnished. A newly created gallery provides a showcase for local artists, a permanent exhibition gives a history resource base for school visits, and Sutton House is home to the Young National Trust Theatre, which, thanks to the support of Barclays Bank, sets out each year to present theatre-in-education in Trust properties throughout the country.

Pupils participating in the Young National Trust Theatre's *Performing Arts in Trust* project at Sutton House.

Uppark

❧

Uppark, perched high on the Sussex Downs, was built in 1690 for Forde, Lord Grey of Werke, an odious man by all accounts, though he created a beautiful house. In 1747 it was bought by Matthew Fetherstonhaugh, who took advantage of an inheritance to furnish the rooms in the latest European fashion and installed his paintings, collected on the Grand Tour. Just over two centuries later, Uppark passed to the National Trust.

The very special quality of the house was that it was so unaltered: through the years furnishings had been repaired, not replaced, contents left unmoved. This repose was rudely shattered on 30 August 1989 when Uppark caught fire during re-roofing work.

While the fire was fought, a salvage operation was mounted by house staff, the donor's family, fire crews, local volunteers and Trust staff. They were able to rescue a remarkably high proportion of the Trust's contents from the showrooms. Much of the interior – panelling, carved wood and plaster, wallpapers and fittings – were also salvaged.

After much debate and assessment of the damage, the Trust decided that conservation was feasible and embarked on a multi-million pound programme, backed by insurance, to restore the house to its appearance before the fire, using as much as possible of the salvaged original material. The result has been a triumph of conservation over tragedy which has reawakened old crafts to match the exceptional quality of the original house with new work and seamless repairs to the old. The contents of the house have been similarly repaired and installed to prepare Uppark for reopening in 1995, with a major exhibition to show what has been achieved.

Above: Uppark, West Sussex, showing the house covered in scaffolding and plastic sheeting following the disastrous fire of 30 August 1989.
Below: Fragments of a chandelier salvaged from the fire at Uppark.

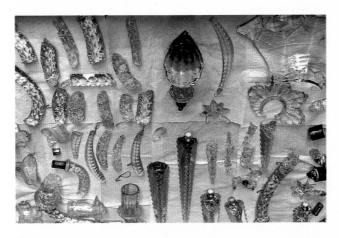

About the National Trust

The National Trust is the leading conservation charity in Europe. It depends entirely for its income on its members and supporters and receives no financial help from the government. It looks after 600,000 acres of countryside, 545 miles of coastline, 230 historic houses and 130 important gardens in England, Wales and Northern Ireland. The Trust continually requires funds to meet its responsibility of preserving the nation's heritage in perpetuity. To find out how you can help, please contact: The National Trust Fundraising Section, 36 Queen Anne's Gate, London SW1H 9AS (0171 222 9251).

MEMBERSHIP

Apart from financial help to the National Trust, membership will give you free admission to properties and various other benefits. For information, contact: The National Trust Membership Department, PO Box 39, Bromley, Kent BR1 1NH (0181 464 1111).

LEGACIES

Please consider leaving the Trust a legacy in your will. All legacies to the National Trust are used either for capital expenditure at existing properties or for the purchase or endowment of new property. None is spent on administration. For further information, contact: The Head of Legacies Unit, 36 Queen Anne's Gate, London SW1H 9AS (0171 222 9251).

THE ROYAL OAK FOUNDATION

This U.S. not-for-profit membership organisation supports the National Trust's activities in areas of special interest to Americans. For membership and programme information in the U.S., contact: Royal Oak, 285 West Broadway, New York, N.Y. 10013 (1-800 913 6565).

A detail of one of the mosaic floors at Chedworth Roman Villa, Gloucestershire.